MERMAID THEORY
POEMS

maya salameh

Haymarket Books
Chicago, IL

© 2026 Maya Salameh

Published in 2026 by
Haymarket Books
P.O. Box 180165
Chicago, IL 60618
773-583-7884
www.haymarketbooks.org
info@haymarketbooks.org

ISBN: 979-888890-652-1

Distributed to the trade in the US through Consortium Book Sales and Distribution (www.cbsd.com) and internationally through Ingram Publisher Services International (www.ingramcontent.com).

This book was published with the generous support of Lannan Foundation, Marguerite Casey Foundation, and Wallace Action Fund.

Special discounts are available for bulk purchases by organizations and institutions. Please email info@haymarketbooks.org for more information.

Grateful acknowledgment is made to the following for permission to reprint materials: "Along the coast to Tripoli. Tripoli. El-Bedoui. Seething mass of 'sacred fish,'" photographed by American Colony (Jerusalem) Photo Department, ca. 1920–1933. Courtesy of the Library of Congress, Prints and Photographs Division, Matson Photograph Collection, LC-DIG-matpc-15436.

Cover design by Margaret Weiner

Printed in the United States.

Library of Congress Cataloging-in-Publication data is available.
Library of Congress Control Number: 2025949188

10 9 8 7 6 5 4 3 2 1

For my mother.

For the first mermaid.

There is no separation between the sea and a woman and it is futile to look further, in thought or through the experience of others, in order to come close to the essence of what is feminine: water, salt, phosphorus, plankton, all the minerals in liquid form.

—Etel Adnan, *Of Cities and Women; Letter from Beirut (August 23rd, 1991)*

Contents

Preface
Pleasure Is Data 3

The Legend Goes That
Aubade with Lobotomized Mountain 7
Excerpts from September's Psychosomatic Effects on Arab Am. Girls IRB Protocol #654781 8
Girl Reviews a Party Dress 9
The First Mermaid Ever Climbs Out the Sea & Tells You She Won't Take You Back 10
Dream Sequence 000000010100100 14
Haptic 15
My Country's Fables Say I Am Devoted 16
Archive Spilled on Entryway 17
Cognates 18
How Love Was Invented 19
GATI.fm 20
Annotated Bibliography 21
Seismograph 23
How to Braid an Artery 25

Estuary/Girl
For Every Siren with a Drill 29
Excerpts from September's Psychosomatic Effects on Arab Am. Girls IRB Protocol #654781 30
Note on Methodology 31
$40 Beige Rico Nasty Tee 32
Haggling the Shami Way 33
Estuary Ghazal (American) 39
Estuary Ghazal (Arab) 40
Anatomy of Gati's Vanity 41
In My Dreams I'm Never Beautiful 42
Analgesic 43

To2borne (May You Bury Me) 44

Gati Visits Victoria's Secret 45

Mitosis 46

Pisces 47

First Blood 48

Mermaid Theory 49

Common Maronite Hymns

Example Sermon 53

Ritual Ethnography 54

Like a Paraphrase for Mortar 56

Elevator to Venus 57

Amtrak Devotional (Why Aren't Y'all Driving Your Friends to the Airport??) 58

The First Mermaid Ever Learns Imperial Units 59

I Wanna Be an Uncle When I Grow Up 60

Staying in Touch with People Who Are Dead. 61

Me & the Jinn in Your Laptop Had a Talk About You 62

Horror Movie Where We Survive 63

Pelvic Ultrasound in July 64

Stations of the Cross 65

As for Beauty, That Bitch with Her Hands in Our Larynx 66

Common Maronite Hymns 68

Music to Drown By 69

Acknowledgments 71

Notes 72

Gratitudes 74

The boundary is permeable between tool and myth, instrument and concept. Indeed, myth and tool mutually constitute each other.

—Donna Haraway, *A Cyborg Manifesto*

Among Syrian Christians, and Muslims, a common way to cope with distress is by prayer... Some Christians, for example, may make a vow that a female family member will wear a special dress (taub el adra, or توب العدرا) for a period of time, if God helps them through their difficulties.

—UNHCR, *Culture, Context and the Mental Health and Psychosocial Wellbeing of Syrians: A Review for Support Staff Working with Syrians Affected by Armed Conflict*

Preface

Pleasure Is Data

a summer Wednesday & my roommates & I drive out to Berkeley   visit Nina in her historic house w/ the wide balcony the trampoline responsible for her roommate's twisted ACL   connive over mango Ices discuss solutions for anemia *Aquarius rights* & the ratio of tops to bottoms &   though we outgrew this discourse in 2012   we still sing Frank Ocean's riff on She   Nina & her friends are still sophomores & haven't had their gender crisis yet   that's for us   the alleged oldheads   pressed into skinny jeans & rope chains   we say her neighborhood feels haunted   she says probably   & my polyester sundress has been praying over my skin for six hours   Atargatis is wearing thrifted Karen Millen but for now she is warm & a little drunk but not so drunk she's worried about her hair & the July has been making her skin glow   earlier we shared a cig outside the Redwood City McDonald's   but it was July & even though some dude was eyeing us like pieces of angus in the white Cadillac by the exit   the air was so damn hot & we were more bored than afraid   the pregame is late & Nina's apartment is crowded with girls us creatures of miniskirts & baggy Carhartts   & we're a morass   lashes drunk with sweat   there was a tear in Gati's trouser seam I traced with my teeth   there is no Arab mermaid unaware of the sound of a Crusader's laugh   I mean war is the death of awe   (among other women)   Soju spilling off the dining table & the liquor makes our cheeks a livid pink   a woman approaches   all diluvian walk   compliments my burgundy pressons they were her high school color   & did I know I was dangerous?   she turns my palms over in her hands   but   it's Wednesday night   the set is perfect   the mojitos suck   the neighborhood's bloomed/corroding & Nina's lacy tank top makes her look resurrected

The Legend Goes That

There was the Mediterranean: you

could walk into the water and stay there.

—June Jordan, *Apologies to All the People in Lebanon*

Aubade with Lobotomized Mountain

my mother refused an epidural so I'd
never mispronounce anything. we drove

past the mountains once &
the radio trembled as if kissed

by static or god. I'm a sharkish girl,
rude mouth, new molars jagged

as cliffs. me & dad sit in the dip
of the Vandross & he tells me about

his city like it doesn't exist or its
neighboring ocean is unemployed. says

shit like in Trablos morning was on everything
& I become an abundance in a thin seat,

asking my catechism teacher do
soldiers go to heaven? if someone

breaks into my house looking for bread
& I panic & hit them with a skillet

which one of us gets punished. who
gets punished? the hospital I was born in

was called Zion. we drive past the mountains
I'm wearing striped shorts & flames

cling to the bluffs like an expensive dress.
I am four. maybe California is my true country.

maybe her fires. I pull a bag of tinted negatives
from my ribs. I was named after water.

Excerpts from September's Psychosomatic Effects on Arab Am. Girls IRB Protocol #654781

INTRODUCTION

resulted in the traumatization of   and raised concerns of
                    specific trauma for Arab Americans. [...] Young Arab women
may be torn about   and the ability to   ,
        especially given

STUDY AIMS & HYPOTHESES

As described above, limited psychological research
and additional scientific attention is warranted in order to
                                        further understand this
community's   and to investigate some of the factors under-
lying   experience a
                    , both sources of formal   therapy, counseling,
or psychiatric medication) or informal   praying,
                    Specifically, this study seeks to

        ;

                    can offer a neglected perspective on

        , broadening clinicians' knowledge and helping to reduce treatment barriers
(Aloud & Rathur, 2009). For the sake of this study, the term Arab
American includes
, regardless of   .

Due to the exploratory nature of this study,   some general primary
hypotheses: 1)
                    ; 2) some or much of symptom experience will vary
from traditionally-validated DSM criteria; and 3)
                            vary by   nativity.

Girl Reviews a Party Dress

    the mauve tone is soooo trendy right now & I wore a medium
        but it fit sort of weird around my shoulders. i weigh

much btw and it's my niece's

                    i wore it for   I was

        gorgeous!

    , especially under a button down.   so comfortable

I ate and walked. My only 2 complaints were

and they smell funny in the dryer. For reference
I got a size 10   I'm 5'2 and 166lb

                        has the LOVELIEST texture

19th bday. I'll be styling it differently than here of
course lol my bad for the mess behind me but th point is it

                      & the light kissed me so well that night
                      I wasn't a girl anymore

The First Mermaid Ever Climbs Out the Sea & Tells You She Won't Take You Back

in the house we speak 3 languages but grooming's the first. baba splays hours shaving his face & smearing cologne on his thorax. mama sits on the toilet, razing her hair of texture from root to tip. me in front of the mirror, knuckles smudged with ash, brows still virgin & thick
&

so Atargatis is a fertility goddess of Northern Syria who accidentally kills her husband while making love to him (pussy too bomb). she's so sad about it that she drowns herself in a lake, but she's so lovely in her drowning the gods transform her into the world's very first mermaid: mossy scales, the slow gait of something lungless. while this goes down, the weather keeps changing & golden hour gets later & later. a toddler complains about her food, a boy asks for a motorcycle, a daughter trims their bangs

&

                                       I emerged from the ocean, all ringlets &
                                      swatched rigging of ribs. I was a girl once.
                         I watched my six, parted my scalp down the middle.
                             I'm a myth now, gleaming opal teeth, talons long
                                   as a trailing thyroid. I'm printed
                                               on coins. professors
                                  allude to me in crowded hallways

&

I climb out of the ocean & my eyes are gorgeous but my gills haven't grown out yet. I walk to the grocery store which hasn't yet been eaten by the recession, doors sighing open like a wife tired of being touched. I buy the 7up cake only Esperanza seemed able to find. I was named after water, raised through drought. baba calls my stalker *the man who shadowed you*. I think I am made of shadows. I drip over the backseat & my abdomen splits at the navel; sweat, sea glass, longing, rust, eels, alphabet

&

Some claim the goddess Dione accompanied by Eros
    plunged into the Euphrates, whereby
    a pair of fish came to guide them
    through the water to aid her escape
    from her husband, god Typhon.
    The fish are commemorated
    as the constellation Pisces, &
    local Syrians apparently abstain
    from eating fish on account of it.
    Certain Syriacs call this Lent.

The name Dione
    was also an epithet
    of Aphrodite/Venus
    herself. So the legend
    has also been told as one of Venus
    casting herself into the Euphrates, then transforming

&

The second myth
    describes the birth of Syrian Venus,
    our Atargatis, as originating in an egg
    which fell into the Euphrates,
    was rolled onto land by fish, & hatched
    in the clutches of doves

&

in the clutches of doves,
regardless of thefrenchthecrusaderstheottomans,
there are pomelos, the smell of gas, standing in San Juan
behind a mother & her daughter
gossiping in matching sarongs. a daughter
is a compromise, just like a country,
meaning I worry about my beauty,
I pay my taxes, eat turkey bacon. I
come from April, humidity & the irrevocable
singing of birds. once,
my sisters had salt for a mouth.

&
beautiful in her drowning, mama cleanses her pulse of its
iron. in the mornings I make sure to take my folate pills so my
skin appears ruddy & bright   peel at my webbing feet

&

An Atargatis relief set in a circular panel,
the bottom part of which is broken off [the
Zodiac Tyche upper block]. There is a crown
over her wavy hair, which falls down the sides
of her head in two long tresses. Over her
right shoulder is a moon.

&

when I ate my first seal, its silk entrails, its thrashing
with the ceremony of a wedding, I wore its spinal cord for weeks. I wore
a veil of seagrass & vertebrae & I prayed
webbed fingers laced. the annals never say
what happened to the body. only that I changed.

&

so beautiful in her drowning   my spirit speaks six languages   wants to build
a television & melt it for broth   I write here   in the crevice across
pandemics   where an unprecedented amount of us   recognize our country
as the massive peach it is   rupturing at the skin with rot   I am so full of salt
so wined & well-fed so American
&

I tried to get Miss Fish Goddess off the table but she keeps yelling
I THINK ROSEWATER IS CURATIVE I
THINK BEAUTY WILL SAVE ME
I'M RUNNING LOW ON BLUE MASCARA &
BETWEEN MY LEGS IS A RIVER

&

on Gati's days off we steal brown lip liners
from Target, binge grape sour patches

& Scandal. we explain our spleens
to the class, like I walk into an antique store

& there is my people's ghost
in a display case next to earrings. we

walk with our backs straight. we've
just dyed our roots red. we know

what is most delicious to animals.

Dream Sequence 000000010100100

we're in a club with six corner rooms the lapis LED bulbs ring
off your new haircut I'm in an indigo dress & the polyester
kisses me just fine. I request Kehlani & you oblige. I wind against
the wood of the awning. mama always said a husband should
make you feel expensive & my dress cost six dollars. there's a molar
that's been pressing against my gums for two weeks but I walk with
the cadence of marrow & your eyes follow me in the mirror. you've
seen me in your reflection, all gall. the nighttime dapples the wall.

Haptic

when I am only a figment of the
war's imagination, when the news
rots my groceries, virus makes
my appendix swell. pin me

to the coral gurney, touch
my enamel. I'll transcribe myself
to bricks. I'll try & find
my way to the bathroom. the

tub is cold, brimming with panic
& lemongrass. on tv you'll button
your fingers together, reeking of
compliance. you'll raise a palm. my

ectoplasm will sing, but my body
won't stop. here, in the aftermath, &
we watch boys eviscerated from press
jackets. we watch the soil grow hard.

My Country's Fables Say I Am Devoted

The six dollar sunflowers we bought after arguing over the cost of raspberries,
        our debates over new cities: Montreal, Ann Arbor, Sydney, Los

Angeles. We measure our navy passports against our marked bodies, practice
        our Spanish, the duskskinned French. Silt & fog & our serrated

        syntax, tongues constellating on the duvet. My country's fables say I am devoted.
The sun slumps against the snipers on the roofs of my university,

        my father's suitcases split at the seam like soft fruit. It's July,
the tile stinks of Lysol. I don't want to buy anything anymore.

Psychology banned in Florida & my country's fables
say I am not endangered. Yes, the poison vowels slicking our floor & my mother

        wanted me to have a neutral name. But sprawl of sticky letters
repeating my refusal, but let me winnow my rage into something of use.

        Let me remain a spell in a long black skirt, stitched incantation of soot,
sap, roe, silk. My dancing means nothing more than dancing & I'm

simmering grasshoppers for protein, breeding chickens in
the backyard. San Diego stays gray forever & romance is dead & oranges

        grow best in deep, well-drained soil & I hear
this music in my food. July & the heat syrups our spines, we stop for gas, you spit

        in the dirt & swear the season will never end.

Archive Spilled on Entryway

we are more than daughters   our mothers
more than prayers   to tell ourselves
at night   one of my grandmothers
was a coiffeuse   sometimes

she visits me in the shower   compels me to pull
my curls w/ the care of a geometrician   ie

her love is thorough   she scrubs my feet with
pumice   ensures my shoulders are lotioned
after showering   ie   cosmology:

in the nursing home   teta split the bedspread
by nine at the latest   & they stored her meals in a
red Tupperware in a shared fridge   in a quiet
neighborhood   where she didn't know anyone's last
name
     I smear tobacco   mutilate
the Canon with my mouth   in one photo

Esperanza in a pink bandanna   floating boleros
across the kitchen   I can see her step off the bus
of the hours   let her lips tint
true mahogany   hum with all her teeth

I like to think that second   was a pool
   a bloom   that didn't demand anything   in my
favorite photo
she's in the yard barefoot   beheading onions
holding a lit cigarette   & berating somebody
     sometimes
my throat opens & all her names spill out

Cognates

I ask you what time for lunch & you smile like
        a word for the end of August. the stanza
                of our slacks imprinted on the desk. I told

your mother I'd make you salmon & I did. of all
        my prayers you are my favorite. you promise
                your palm into my stomach. a month ago

we sat in the middle of a park advocating our
        hearts & it was 3 o'clock & your eyes were
                the shape of clouds. it's November now

& the noun under the sink is screaming again
        but we couldn't care less, your feet planted
                shoulder width between my ankles. your

hands leave zinnias on my legs & we're learning
        control is the opposite of love. I want to wait
                on you to get home, match on Halloween.

How Love Was Invented

a girl meets a girl & they become a quadratic, a proof. a girl meets a girl & parabola of her back at noon, comorbidities of their legs twined together. a girl meets a girl & becomes a biome, a biology with no grammar. biome: how my hair ends up in your food. throughout our marry me chicken with the sundried tomatoes. biome: your hands above my ovaries, rubbing me to sleep. your clutching the glass damn near dropped, the dish washer's song I forgot to play, the email you were anxious to write, the candles I always light. laying around, orbits touching on a Sunday night, hair arrayed neatly in scarves, noses bumping as we laugh. when a girl & a girl love each other, they make an elegy. this song lasts longer than the mountains & all the horses nearby can smell it.

GATI.fm

> *bitch, I still don't know how to drive! but I*
> *made a fandroid outta your girlfriend.*
>
> *I learned this word on*
> *Rihanna's internet. for a while I was*
>
> *boyish like foxes were &*
> *the aunties called it sophisticated*
> *& I've never been sixteen before*
>
> *, just sistered. I used to sleep in the Mediterranean*
> *where there were no Tigris girls*
> *with my language under the rubble, just*
>
> *those in my dialect who joined*
> *my sea sometimes. we sleep there & it's*
> *good sleep, uninterrupted by presidents.*
>
> *my tongue split as an eel's, fluent*
> *in peat & phosphorous & all the gossip*
> *seeping from drowned cellphones. my voice*
> *fogs over mirrors, makes children*
> *wander from bed.*
>
> *I cross-validate scales*
> *with my blood & the dying*
> *is dazzling on me,*
> *innovated. all I'm asking*
>
> *is to borrow yr flat iron*
> *for a couple hours.*
> *listen. I was a girl once. I have legs now*
> *& I speak maroon. listen. I'm*
>
> *trying to trap you in this archive. I am*
> *trying to commemorate this serve.*

Annotated Bibliography

I watched her murder on my phone
on the way to the airport. Somewhere

in a minefield, a sign is missing. The skeleton
of this absence is very old. For many journalists,

Arab life is worthless. For many investors,
Arab death is worth a lot. Every time

phenotype makes another machinic connection,
there is a stutter. On October 6, 2023, the value

of a Lockheed Martin share was $402. Today,
they're worth $603. Every theory

is a burial. Legibility is neither the end goal
nor a stable, infinite state. In Arabic

the word for "story" is riwaya, and " to narrate"
is tirwa, from rawa—this is the same root—

the same word—for "to water, irrigate."
To narrate is to irrigate. The Mediterranean

is a vast archive, an immense grave. Who
will pay for all this access? I stood there

at the doorway of the story
where I waited and waited.

Seismograph

my hands stutter like hummingbirds over skin,

I fiddle with the Ticonderoga's chewed up pink head. the exam flakes

beauty is a technology. exile is a spectrum.

how am I. where have I been. I am always

&

you ask me to use sunflower oil. but I'm saying loneliness will come for you, if you allow it.

there was an empty bench for us & my fingernails

were painted turquoise.

, the kind of mystery that is a sacrament.

at the end of dinner we walk back to the car. you thumb my palm.

you ask do we need to buy parsley for tomorrow.

we are coastal & mountainous, I am fanged & irrational. but we sleep well & honestly, with no jaw pains. (3ishq.)

like a girl who has never done this before.

ameen.

How to Braid an Artery

     : I laugh with the velocity of pigskin, discuss god with boys I will never see again.
we toss languages around the table like we remember them, hull a sunflower skeleton with
our eyes:

     :: an event
is just a set of things. a Sunday ago, I:

     : the street spills over our tired necks, my brother scratches his script into
tree stomach. my body: preceded

     : me by three centuries at least. the city sculpts a screenplay out of
us, sidewalk promising summers we may not survive to drink. Aleppo's back hums
when she sits down:

     : I remember the city as a demarcation, or a divot in coffee:
     : it was never about hagiography. it was about my tombstone & writing something
different on it:

     : a year ago I kept canisters of similes in my basement. I
watch our boys become soldiers
every night. I eat the music that makes me old again: my brother:

     : recites the pavement with me, too busy to notice the varicose veins in
the asphalt:

     :: tell me how Aleppo taught me yardage, listened to me stretch, eat. I braid
the sameness with which we bleed, arrange the tolls on my wall like linebackers: tell me
how I gurgle these letters, the dead's grammar, the dead:

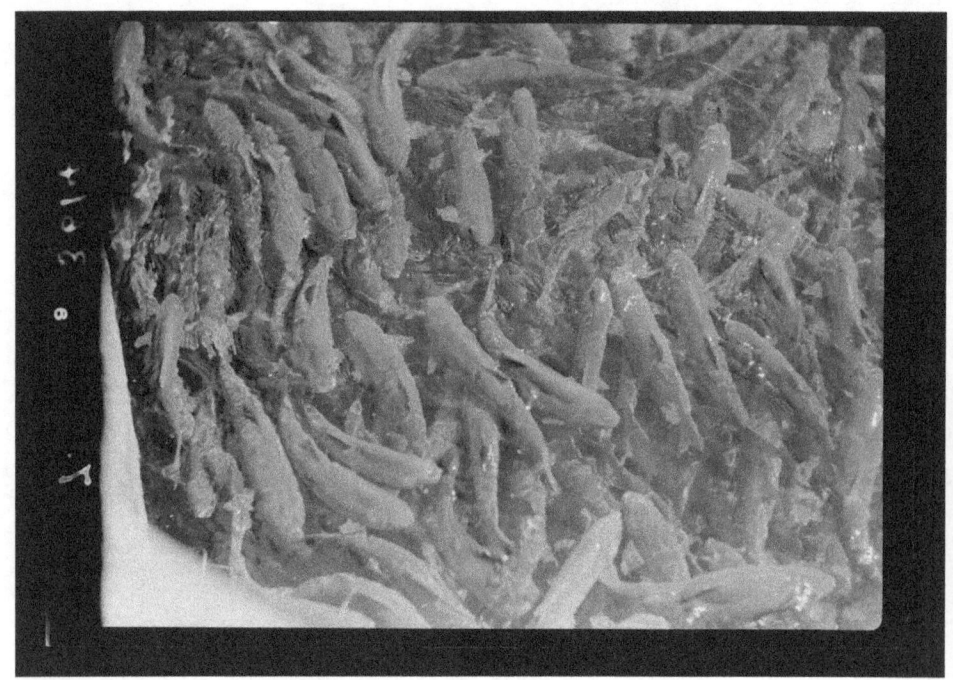
Seething mass of sacred fish along the coast to Tripoli (1933).

Estuary/Girl

≋

Aren't these shores

an open book of history?

—Oskar Flatt, *The Banks of the Wisła*

For Every Siren with a Drill

& god bless the nail techs /
the girls pressing their acrylics to yours
or blotting concealer in shared apartments / to

whom you admit you find
your fingers wide & mannish / the ones
who say yup, Catholic dads lol / this was how I hid

tank tops under jackets: / thank
you @setsbym thank you Ida from the
wax joint on Adams Avenue / your new man sounds

like a better father than your last
& your skin really does glow when you're
in love / thank you Arwa who on occasional Saturdays

I can convince to henna me / bless
the coconut oil you prescribe my ink / bless
our shared hymns / girlhood passed with loving

instructions / the roommate who taught me
diffusing & the best bath & body works flavor /
cherry blossom / you file my thumbs into blades /

pull my hair from its follicles / we launder
my knotted parts / & for the next three hours /
our mouths / are stained with the same longing

Excerpts from September's Psychosomatic Effects on Arab Am. Girls IRB Protocol #654781

SCALES

RATE YOUR LEVEL OF ACTIVITY.

☐ 1 ☐ 2 ☐ 3 ☐ 4 ☐ 5 ☐ 6 ☐ 7 ☐ 8 ☐ 9 ☐ 10

RATE YOUR UNEASE.

☐ 1 ☐ 2 ☐ 3 ☐ 4 ☐ 5 ☐ 6 ☐ 7 ☐ 8 ☐ 9 ☐ 10

HOW OFTEN DO YOU EAT?

☐ never ☐ once daily ☐ twice daily ☐ three times daily ☐ four times or more daily

PARTICIPANT SURVEY

- how often do you line your eyes?
- how would you describe your appetite?
- can I look?
- which famine do you belong to?
- where is your mother?
- would you describe yourself as an optimistic person?
- how often does your tide come?
- does the shelling pattern your blood?
- will you watch your mouth?
- where are her sons?
- how old is your fatigue?
- your mouth?
- can I look?

Note on Methodology

if I slipped over the seafloor like a duvet
thumbed its creases
I'd find plastic & kinfolk & anglerfish
I'd find proof of my doomedness

$40 Beige Rico Nasty Tee

H & their ravenous love for life their smile warmer than Henny their sideways wink   it's August & the antidepressants are working   I beam in my dress rife with abrasions   slices of my hips & ribs   shining from the slits   I bruise so easy & it's almost the end of summer you can taste it on everyone's voices & H has a way of making me playful again teasing me into venturing out of the new apartment   we christen the bathroom with smoke   have pleasant conversations with our mothers on the phone   gossip about the church daughters like we aren't them   outside sirens ring but the fire isn't us & H has a way of admitting things that makes you want to love them   they explain how to cook a seafood boil without letting the corn dry out   we discuss our mothers & they're more women than ghosts   & we're more boys than daughters   grinning & walking slow at the Kehlani concert   we worship at her outfit the color of slate   surrounded by other church daughters   when we finally get back home all we need is the washed sheets   the gray camp chair on the balcony   the quasi-quiet of insects at night   merch cost $40 & the train was late but   most shit can be fixed if you put a little Old Bay on it

Haggling the Shami Way

The week after my college graduation, our family returns to Syria. We fly into the Beirut airport because Israel's bombed the one in Damascus again.[1] I buy gummy Skittles and pop a cloud every hour we ferment at the southern border: lemon, blueberry, lime, red. Baba didn't bring our birth certificates or acquire us visas, and our swollen faces don't serve as sufficient proof of Sham. We spend our first morning in the homeland driving to Kafroun, jiddo's village; spanning the roads are long blades of grain, crucifixes in the ground, checkpoints upon checkpoints tilled by men who are boys still. Jiddo introduces my brother and I to his fig trees, his plums, the vineyard he's devised on the roof. He walks us to the creek sourced from the river descended from the mountains. The rocks are slick with moss and cigarette butts.

*

In my mother's childhood home I find pictures of her with hair dyed russet and piled high, eyes lined with kohl, all the attitude of a woman no one's called mama yet. I look at her now returning with American dollars and unhennaed roots and her children who speak with the hesitation of tourists. She is about five foot four. When she leans over the sink to rinse rice, her shoulder blades poke through her shirt like prayer wings. Down the street, mama's cousin tells us about her husband, shot in his study eighteen months ago. She folds her hands the way widows do, describes the hole in his occipital bone and the *mabrouks* which littered her son from 2012 on. Martyrdom was still rare at that point in the war. Her eyes don't glimmer. They are a river with no source.

By the fourth day of our return, finally in Damascus, my sister and I wake up sick as dogs. I convince Baba to buy me an anklet even though he's scared they're for ra'assat because *do I look like a dancer? I just got my master's* and his friend discounts the silver. Baba turns a soft red in the sun. His mercury fillings click when he eats fruit. We stroll through the souk and each vendor appraises us gram for gram. Only mom really walks with Sham in it. My temples protest the entire first week while I romanticize Palo Alto's clinical organization, the wide roads and campus lawns trimmed like spreadsheet cells. I miss my girls and my boxy room. On Father's Day I throw up and buy another anklet, this time with small beads

---

1 'Heavy' damage to Damascus airport confirmed after Israeli attack, Al Jazeera (Jun. 11, 2022), https://www.aljazeera.com/news/2022/6/11/syria-says-significant-damage-to-airport-from-israeli-strike.

tinted like variegated lilies. Lots more 7UP. Baba says it is essential to witness others' pain.

*

By the second week, the rhythm of our days softens. Around dusk my sister puts on her long velvet dress and finally I rise from our shared bed and tweeze the side of my face, preen with the blue liner I bought. A sister's beauty is contagious like that. Crushed velvet frames her lovely fair skin which everyone here comments on. Rayon the color of sky showcases my less fair skin everyone comments on. The two of us as girls, baidah w samra. Baidah w samra still, we share a vodka cranberry, ignore that last night we fought over the last of the hot water, the largest towel in the linoleum bathroom. Tonight we're quiet, leaning toward each other in the gold light, passing the green hookah hose back and forth. We gaze at the Mediterranean which taught us to swim. I was four, Baba dropped me in the water, I learned to tread, and the water was the widest thing I've ever been taught. In my chest wasps, moths, timid flies.

*

Everyone loves older men and even older cities. But women / must be girls, and preferably girls from out of town. But / I've lived here my whole life.

—Sennah Yee

*

The locust is a species resistant to extermination.[2] I am a phylum of my own, extinct for six hundred years already. Participant background: the skin of my killer is seated first on airplanes, especially when their navy uniform is starched. In sunny San Diego where I grow up, most of the men who approach me are soldiers. They try impressing me with new white Chevy Silverados, free college, the wide pensions the ROTC kids in calculus class count, ripe fruit of a long will cashed on bodies like mine. My hometown is nicknamed America's Finest City and the weather looks real good and so do the men.

In another timeline, I don't need to explain my blood to the handsome scientist.

---

2 In 1926, French and British mandate authorities reached an agreement with Turkey to prevent locust swarms in Syria. The agreement founded an International Bureau to fight locusts, based in Damascus. *See* Idir Ouahes, *French Mandate Syria and Lebanon: Land, Ecological Interventions, and the "Modern" State*, in Environments of Empire: Networks and Agents of Ecological Change 61, 68 (Ulrike Kirchberger & Brett Bennett eds., Univ. of North Carolina Press 2020).

No crusaders rolling, pushing, and developing my corpse towards California, long arc of history explaining the chronic conditions on my university intake form. I'm a good animal.³ I'm well vaccinated, compliant, complaining of womb aches migraines moroseness. I sear lamb, brown broccoli heads in the skillet. I want to write down this maroon haunt I've inherited, the thing that blooms behind my molars when someone says home like it's a clean word. I want to pin it against the wall and make indentations in its back with my nails. But I've painted them cream and they glow in the dark and I think that would frighten a cryptid of that size.

For now it's still Damascus, we've hit our third week, I start assimilating. We spend our days visiting kin, shuttling from apartment to apartment, the fountains in the hotels we can't afford ancient and creamy marble. On every street, the sound of too-young children selling roses. Most are unaccompanied. Teta asks me if I've ever been in love while I cut my hair in the mirror. We stand in the bathroom together while she paints her lids gold. This is the best language we have in common. We gossip about the other church girls and how غ ر's daughter is two thirds of last summer's weight. The night falls on us around nine and I start reclining into my Arabic, its skirts molding to my palms. On the second floor of our hotel, all the rooms are reserved for UNRWA workers that never come. Their signage eyesores the lobby. No AC so I listen to the music of cicadas while I wait for the heat to abate so I can sleep. I am molting, but I don't mind. I want something ancient to touch me back.

The next day, on a morning blurry with humidity, we visit the Bimaristan al-Nuri in al-Hariqa, one of the oldest hospitals in the world. It has a stone archway with a sultan's name carved above it and my palms touch cold muqarnas. At the center of the courtyard is a fountain meant to calm patients. The walls have craters in them from unknown combatants. Here, illness was treated with enough to eat, music, spiritual and somatic treatments. I try to believe kindness once lived here as policy. I try to believe someone once left cured. I touch the inscriptions in the stone and think this is what I hope my children inherit, rooms echoing with the footfalls of students, diagrams of the nervous system, the free healing of strangers. It smells of cedar and antiseptic.

---

3   PBS NewsHour, *UN Commission Accuses Israel of Genocide in Gaza: Lawyers Offer Opposing Views on Findings* (Sept. 17, 2025), https://www.pbs.org/newshour/show/un-commission-accuses-israel-of-genocide-in-gaza-lawyers-offer-opposing-views-on-findings (citing Israeli Defense Minister Yoav Gallant's Oct. 9, 2023 declaration that "We are fighting human animals and we are acting accordingly").

*

The first language I practice upon my return to America is the body. I am back where the roads are smooth and the grief is neater, more quiet. I listen to Tiny Desks stoned. I cook breakfast in the sunny sublet, dice green onions. I try putting myself to sleep by hand, by reading. But my sternum emits jasmine and petrol, my body for weeks dehydrated like it remembers its nativity. Back there, over there, over my body, Israel bombs the airport in Damascus three times. Israel pokes its heels into the Golan. Israel rots my grandmother's food in her fridge. The war is over but it's not. It's changed skins and tactics.

*

No ocean, however tumultuous it may be, can give us an idea more exact (and moving) of water than does the smallest little stream in the gardens of Damascus.

—Etel Adnan

*

In Baba's hometown, Tripoli, Beirut's cousin with more tattered skirts, we bicker in the chalet, the restaurant, walking past the gutted construction projects with pink bougainvillea climbing their ribs. I snip at my sister over the adapter we have to share because I'm the only one who remembered to buy one. Before breakfast I lecture my little brother about astrology, how height-increasing insoles are in fact a red flag. I offer him sun and moon and rising. We give our birth times to my algorithm, wall in piles around the bed. The chalet has no working doors but the pool is rich cerulean and eight feet deep. The air in Trablos is briny and generous and the dumpsters throughout the city remain saturated as loam, just the same as in 2015, though the pollution's worse and more fish are poisonous to eat. It is important to witness. The gutters glimmer with diesel. My witnessing teems from my throat and my belly.

While we drive to the Hallab store filled with cantaloupe ice cream, 2ashta ice cream, mulberry ice cream, we argue about who is responsible for the roads being closed off. Mom's friend accuses the Americans, my grandmother the Russians, and mom's sister's neighbor blames the Kurds. Baba wanted to take us to Palmyra, but the cab driver says the route there from the border is still controlled by ISIS. I'm not sure how to write about this without sounding Orientalist. At the risk of being a native informant about the circumstances of my life, at the risk of sounding Orientalist, at the risk of sounding American, at the risk of sounding Arab, at the risk of sounding alive— the facts don't save us. But they might say we lived.

*

These were the facts: I was the eldest daughter of a Syrian mother and Lebanese father, born the August before 9/11. I started kindergarten speaking mostly Arabic. I spent every summer in Damascus until 2011. I started high school watching White boys debate it and our women kept disappearing. Our women kept piling into boats headed to Greece and no one looked for them.[4] I live twenty minutes now from the Pacific. Baba didn't want to leave Lebanon. A car bomb went off across the street from him. He almost died. He got a scholarship from a university in Michigan. He worked as: a grocery store bagger, a chauffeur, a dog walker, and a car parts assembler. He screwed the handles on the doors of shiny new Fords. He earned his doctorate in psychology. He wrote his dissertation about humor. When he moved to San Diego, he avoided the Pacific. He told us the Mediterranean was too beautiful. He told us America was good to him. In his free time, Baba collects coins. Somewhere, the cryptid is growing wings.

*

It's June in Damascus and no poetry can equal it. The souk ceiling is the color of charcoal, it is addled with bullet holes. Mama still barters like she's Shami, arguing unnecessarily over the cost of each smell we take home: ward, yasmeen, dara2. Long covid has emaciated my smelling ability but the tinted oils still work as protective armor. In Palo Alto, and Damascus, and Beirut, I grieve minutiae. I wear the notched black blouse mama said made me look like an angel. Mama whose moods bloomed like bruises across our days. I dream of bumping into her on the way to the bathroom without flinching. Coming home to her screaming or laughing *you forgot to take the chicken out.*[5]

It's mid-August now and mama's imbued with the current disease, refusing any more medicine. My brother and father are asymptomatic. On FaceTime, I watch my exponentiating brother make our father eggs, his promise of shoulders hunched over the stove. Mama who sleeps on the floor for her discs, turning down amoxicillin. Maybe the pain is exonerating. Maybe another language in common. In my studies, I've learned that keeping secrets is actually very bad for your health. Like causes autoimmune conditions. I recite all the cities hidden in my throat. Boston/

---

[4] Ahmet Gençtürk, *Over 30,000 Migrants Died, Went Missing in Mediterranean: Rights Group Sea Watch International blames EU's isolationist policy for soaring death toll*, Anadolu Agency (Jul. 25, 2024), https://www.aa.com.tr/en/europe/over-30-000-migrants-died-went-missing-in-mediterranean-rights-group/3285118.
[5] Doechii, *Yucky Blucky Fruitcake* (Top Dawg Ent. 2020) at 1:54.

Grass Valley/Trablos/San Juan, tucked neatly beneath my diaphragm. Sixteen and riddled with MRIs, recommendations for counseling, Saint John's wort, birth control. What ends up solving the migraines is Massachusetts, a damp rain from two Augusts ago, Victoria's cherry-red Altima and playing Summer Walker until we believed we were young again.

*

In the last week of our trip, in Lattakia while trying desperately to ignore everybody, I joke with the sun, trade secrets with the sea in the way which extends my life. I find sweetness in the mahogany desks engraved with mother of pearl at the silver market, the geometry of speckled cement making the 3abbasiyeen, the etchings on balconies. I think no one can really understand grief unless their mother spoke Arabic.

Part of it is smoking lavender and chamomile and roses. Burning the things you'd boil for me, mama. Repeating to myself: control is the opposite of love. Control is the opposite of love. Sometimes, the drought picks me up from school. Sometimes I'm thirteen again, listening for the melody of floor submitting to feet. Most days it's three o'clock and I'll be hungry for jerky or fruit or worried I'm not just ovulating or trying to prove I'm not a trousered swarm of bees. But there's still eating a pomegranate with all of your hands and learning to listen to yourself takes a long time. Long ago we crawled out of the water. We can't go back. The chalet has perforated walls. I stare at my phone with my volume off. I try to mime the words I love you.

Estuary Ghazal (American)

Got to   love us American 3arab, all singing blue sea
is holiest   from our own steel church basins, wringing true sea

from auntie's dre   sses in Beirut, we humanimals living
in the belly of our   apex predator, drinking new sea,

building para-wadis in   our bedrooms using statues
of the Virgin, our estuaries   only bringing crude sea

to rivers, we're telling you that   the dead are in the water,
they have become an enviro   nment, no more stinging blue sea

left for the living or the   drowned, here reminding you the
Mediterranean is a long   grave, clinging tattoo sea

of lost cousins, that   dear America & her daughters
are looking, thoughts   & prayering, sirens ringing, cue sea.

Estuary Ghazal (Arab)

Maybe the longest poem I can   write is the slow river
in jiddo's village which I   won't name, though thrushes of vetiver,

though a wide blue pa   ssport, despite my fluency, despite
my countries kissing   on watchlists, though my mother stows myrrh

between her leggings,   though my telling this story is never
innocent, though our   killer has made flour & dough a blur

of girls' clothing, that   my name derives from water but now means
I'm from a long drown   ing, the murder of cedars, bough & fir,

that it doesn't   matter what I want, that I am a partially
enclosed body of   water connected from fallow river

to sea, that I   am a body which still remembers every
shallow grave   I've been found in, my birthmarks, sallow liver & all.

Anatomy of Gati's Vanity

in the reef I keep:
    {VECTOR} coins
    {VECTOR} inherited silver
    {VECTOR} the necklaces of young girls
    {VECTOR} Kiko Milano 3d Hydra Lipgloss 32 | Brun Rose
    {VECTOR} 15,000 tons of crude oil[6]
    {VECTOR} 6 cans of 7up
    {VECTOR} Maybelline Precise All Day Smudge Proof Eyeliner, Forest Brown
    {VECTOR} 2 Sparrow target missiles
    {VECTOR} the bones of a Hyundai
    {VECTOR} desire

---

6 In July 2006, an oil slick resulted from Israeli bombing of the power station in Jiyyeh just south of Beirut; its storage tanks seeped 15,000 tons of oil into the sea, the largest-ever oil spill in the already threatened, polluted and dying Mediterranean sea. Munira Khayyat, *A Landscape of War: Ecologies of Resistance and Survival in South Lebanon* at 65 (Univ. of Cal. Press 2022).

In My Dreams I'm Never Beautiful

I'm morning: I'm illuminated: I'm illustrated
at length in the next chapter!
:: the amoxicillin walls & I'm eleven
in front of our shared family desktop

reading the dirtiest fanfiction you can imagine.
I'm a girl again ::& nothing hungry
has ever happened to me.
I'm mourning: I'm illuminated: I'm this fine

the first take. I'm this fine
with a soft beat. my gender
is the way numbers kiss letters
to make Arabic :: in the dream

there are bags & bags of psalms to pack
& we are late for our flight. there is
a long escalator requiring climbing:
in the service of beauty I

replace one stud with another then
my nose gets too pink so I get nervous
& switch it back. in Boston I trim my bangs,
conduct what I call hairline surgery:: is

really just tweezing my jawline clean. (please.
give me something to do with my hands.)
I'm morning: I'm seventeen, still innocent
of steering wheels. I'm mourning: I'm illuminated:

I'm illustrated at length
in the manual. don't worry.
I'll make my own music.

Analgesic

In Arabic the name of frankincense is cognate
with the name of Lebanon. A man offers a kidney

to feed his children. When people harvest myrrh, they
wound the trees repeatedly, bleed them of the gum.

To2borne (May You Bury Me)

تقبرني تقبرني تقبرني تقبرني تقبرني تقبرني تقبرني تقبرني تقبرني تقبرني تقبرني تقبرني
تقبرني تقبرني تقبرني تقبرني تقبرني تقبرني تقبرني تقبرني تقبرني تقبرني تقبرني تقبرني
تقبرني تقبرني تقبرني تقبرني تقبرني تقبرني تقبرني تقبرني تقبرني تقبرني تقبرني تقبرني
تقبرني تقبرني تقبرني تقبرني تقبرني تقبرني تقبرني تقبرني تقبرني تقبرني تقبرني تقبرني
تقبرني تقبرني تقبرني تقبرني تقبرني تقبرني تقبرني تقبرني تقبرني تقبرني تقبرني تقبرني
تقبرني تقبرني تقبرني تقبرني تقبرني تقبرني تقبرني تقبرني تقبرني تقبرني تقبرني تقبرني
تقبرني تقبرني تقبرني تقبرني تقبرني تقبرني تقبرني تقبرني تقبرني تقبرني تقبرني تقبرني
تقبرني تقبرني تقبرني تقبرني تقبرني تقبرني تقبرني تقبرني تقبرني تقبرني تقبرني تقبرني
تقبرني تقبرني تقبرني تقبرني تقبرني تقبرني تقبرني تقبرني تقبرني تقبرني تقبرني تقبرني
تقبرني تقبرني تقبرني تقبرني تقبرني تقبرني تقبرني تقبرني تقبرني تقبرني تقبرني تقبرني
تقبرني تقبرني تقبرني تقبرني تقبرني تقبرني تقبرني تقبرني تقبرني تقبرني تقبرني تقبرني
تقبرني تقبرني تقبرني تقبرني تقبرني   أقدني   تقبرني تقبرني تقبرني تقبرني
تقبرني تقبرني تقبرني   تقبرنو تقبرني تقبرني تقبرني
تقبرني تقبرني تقبرني   قبرني   تقبرنو تقبرني تقبرني تقبرني
تقبرني تقبرني تقبرني   قبرني   تقبرنو تقبرني تقبرني تقبرني
تقبرني تقبرني تقبرني   قبرني   تقبرنو تقبرني تقبرني تقبرني
تقبرني تقبرني تقبرني   قبرني   تقبرنو تقبرني تقبرني تقبرني
تقبرني تقبرني تقبرني   قبرني   تقبرنو تقبرني تقبرني تقبرني
تقبرني تقبرني تقبرني   قبرني   تقبرنو تقبرني تقبرني تقبرني
تقبرني تقبرني تقبرني تقبرني تقبرني تقبرني تقبرني تقبرني تقبرني تقبرني تقبرني تقبرني
تقبرني تقبرني تقبرني تقبرني تقبرني تقبرني تقبرني تقبرني تقبرني تقبرني تقبرني تقبرني
تقبرني تقبرني تقبرني تقبرني تقبرني تقبرني تقبرني تقبرني تقبرني تقبرني تقبرني تقبرني
تقبرني تقبرني تقبرني تقبرني تقبرني تقبرني تقبرني تقبرني تقبرني تقبرني تقبرني تقبرني
تقبرني تقبرني تقبرني تقبرني تقبرني تقبرني تقبرني تقبرني تقبرني تقبرني تقبرني تقبرني
تقبرني تقبرني تقبرني تقبرني تقبرني تقبرني تقبرني تقبرني تقبرني تقبرني تتقبرني

Gati Visits Victoria's Secret

my cup size is
ventricles innards bones
mismatched socks keys red
chapstick earring backs yellow
candles cinnamon. I want to be Love
Island pretty. the doctors don't know what
to do with me.

Mitosis

                    my desire & my fear sit next to each other
                    in Spanish class. my desire, thick & fuchsia,
                    sits my fear down for dinner. my fear reeks
                    of camellias & lilies. they share a chardonnay,
                    discuss the television. my fear & desire fuck.

I know my fear & desire
would sit on a porch, thick &   my desire is tall down
fuchsia, fear wouldn't discuss the   for dinner. my desire makes a damn
nighttime for the rest of their   good omelet. my fear is
marriage. desire's clots are violet.   dashing in teal, & I am so young.
my fear is green.   we braid our limbs at night.

Pisces

I live near a forest with deer. In January, I saw a wolf chasing a deer while driving.
Wolves are associated with Pisces, Virgos deer. The deer called the cops on the wolf.

Nov 9, 2023, 10:42 PM. 60th email

In freshman year, when I am still a girl, I meet
a quiet boy in my dorm. We say hellos in passing

in the dining hall. He is two years older, maybe.
A year after my graduation, I get a private

message on Twitter. In a month, 600 pages of
devotionals about me, of me, to me. I visit

the police station 7 times in a year. I visit them
more than the dentist. Officer asks am I sure

I didn't sleep with him. In Santa Clara, Torrance,
San Diego. I keep his emails in a folder. I skim

them occasionally to make sure he isn't feeling
violent. I live just south of Night, rife with

clouds, inherited suspicion of pills. I'm safer
as a myth than a woman. August 28 & another

email. I scrub my address from the Internet. I eat
a healthy dinner, imagine being the flesh of two

fish. I dream of being ichthyic, being a symbol
held close to a woman's neck for protection. I

think how easy it is now to take me by the neck.
Officer says not a specific enough intent to kill.

First Blood

in my junior year of college   my two best friends & I visit the gun range
the parking lot is full of trucks with *let's go brandon* stickers on them   their owners
all Midwestern fifty-somethings who ogle us   while we try on our glasses   we press
our index fingers against metal & a current is made   I go last & my shoulders ring
from the impact   I hear my mother's voice   the rifle her teachers put in her
hands   *in case of Israel*   I dream of the girls writing numbers on their wrists
in case of Israel   my mother was 13 years old   she had at least had
her first blood   she could recognize it

Mermaid Theory

Jonah arrived in a whale.
well, I told the driving instructor,
I kissed English for two years before my teacher
believed it. my Arabic was honest liquid / well water.
well, I told the instructor, my mother poured Euphrates
into me & I've been waiting to run out of blood since. Jonah
was the name of the driver, the officiant, the drowned. sometimes
praying is just talking to yourself in the dark.[7]

---

[7] listen ⁓⁓ teta read tea leaves & I can't read much. ⁓ I have a baptismal name ⁓ listen ⁓ Jonah arrived in a whale ⁓ listen ⁓ I was named. lama katia rana rosa maha josephine. ⁓⁓ I'll teach my girls to grow legs & gills ⁓ to speak the fluvial language that will connect them to their village's water source ⁓ listen ⁓ the sea held our bodies & sometimes let them go ⁓ I press my ear to the shore & hear innards ⁓ I press my ear to the shore & am reminded I survived ⁓ the first mermaid was a woman ⁓ whose body was born again from salt ⁓ listen ⁓ who do you love ⁓ how will you save them? ⁓ our women press on theory's heels ⁓ our method spans time & desire & starfish ⁓ our method is we refuse to forget ⁓ our method is it's been summer for years & our hair flows from our napes ⁓ like blue down the mountain. ⁓ I'll teach my girls to know every river that raised them ⁓ our calves riddled with kelp like diacritic marks ⁓ our ankles bloom small silt bruises & our insistence shatters terrors, textbooks, the policies replete with lead. listen ⁓ Jonah arrived ⁓ I was named. ⁓ listen ⁓ this brackish page is crowded ⁓ listen ⁓ where will you go after this poem

Common Maronite Hymns

≋

Can you be water?

One day you will be

that kind of divine.

—Fady Joudah, *[...]*

Example Sermon

& who hasn't dreamed of absolution, of [ECCLESIASTES],
of untimid girls who'd array me in their backseat & teach
me the dictionary of a mouth, sibilance of penitence or spit?
we must remember the Lord, praise Him, blesses us with
[LEVITICUS] thick as fistfuls of February, purple horizon crackling
above our scalps like aluminum in a microwave, like the Lord
was trying to cook us clean. catechism taught me my body, fit me
in my un-Sundayed dress. saffron & myrrh the shape of this liturgy:
the Lord has open hands & loves little wraiths like us, the smell of
sugar burning, the leaven bread we break for our dead. the minor
prophets, the gas station saints, the neglected apostles, the Lord
has [CORINTHIANS] stuffed in his pockets for them, & there is
enough for everyone to eat. beloveds, my longest relation with the
Lord is through begging. someone opens a Snapple & says behold,
this too is my blood. I am not here to confess. I am here holding the
testimony of our living, the dented psalm of it, your hair in my
mouth, freedom is hard work. the apples you eat to the core of.

Ritual Ethnography

> With so many dissonances in my life I have learned actually to prefer being not quite right and out of place. —Edward Said

i. the belly is documentation.	WARNING: this product contains nicotine. nicotine is an addictive chemical.	
ii. throughout my heartbreak I eat like a bird: harvest moon, tobacco, grapefruits, quarter of a frozen pizza, orange blossom syrup.	a. grandma visited last night & said everything would be alright.	b. the belly is documentation. the women in my family are renowned for forgetting.
a. my childhood home flooded last September. my apartment full of smoke this open January.		i. at least my addiction is one I can touch.
iv. a day comes & things start tasting again.	a. my illness isn't a book. it doesn't have a grammar. but I notice women gossiping in chairs against a red wall, taste the clink of my earrings as I close an old door.	b. I still say bism al salib when I wave lavender over my bed because who am I to deny myself the only god I have in Arabic? I am at my most fertile age.
v. I'm happy in Walmart buying omega 3 supplements & warm white LEDs & I burn tobacco in Esperanza's altar until she is fed.	a. the bible asks why should you die before your time? it is right.	
c. ask the doctor: *is my uterus compostable? & who the fuck took my pearls?*		vi. my perfume smells of everything: the narcoleptic mangoes I throw out of the fridge, her perfect teeth.

vii. god's bad at picking up the phone but leaves voicemails often. I saw god at the Bryson Tiller concert & she didn't remember you.	*Abana llazee fee'l samawat Lee yata-kaddas ismooka, Lee ya3'tee ma-la-koo-tooka, Lee takon mashee'atooka kama fee el sama' kaza-lee-ka 3ala el ard Ameen*	
		viiii. I bought a new sun cream for almost $13 & A asked do you have to try everything? & I said I'm my longest poem.
	vii. the reports say the massacres will stay in my diaphragm or my thyroid. but I will not be a monument. I write it down anyway. I refuse to be brief.	
viii. an apocalypse of girls in a cramped campus studio & our conversation smears the room. at midnight's torso we clack past each other in dangly earrings & ribbed tops all conspiring towards dancing, glancing over strangers, sweating our clusters off.	v. I'll write us a new skin, another ocean to cross. I'll write us a boat.	viiii. the women in my family are renowned for forgetting. on Sundays I wear blue, eat lemon loaf cake, listen to the aunties gossip like they still have sons.
	a. mama says egg yolks are auspicious & okra helps your hair grow & god loves women who make their own luck.	

Like a Paraphrase for Mortar

slip
of the silk
nightgowns
Nina & I begged
mama to buy us
in Damascus,
how arduously
we fought
for those ill-fitting
dresses. two months
later us on the phone
laughing about
exes, debating
a friend. hers
was white
& mine navy.
neither fit.

Elevator to Venus

for Sarah Hegazi

this time, I stay, weight
of the entire graphite
sky above us. I clean
willow green ramekins.
we listen for the songs
of frogs. umbilical
things thrush like this,
mispronounced. I want
the lace stitching of doily
we call horizon. *f7emt?* I
want sky. sky. sky. sky.
sky. sky. sky. sky. sky. your
smile predicts rain. next
door Venus is accessible
by elevator & my canines
are on the dresser. *f7emt?*
our name translates
into morning.

Amtrak Devotional
(Why Aren't Y'all Driving Your Friends to the Airport??)

love is inconvenience   waking up at 6am to drive your best friend to court & all the way back out to San Jose for the tacos she loves after   arguing red or green sauce in a sticky vinyl booth   sitting on the amtrak for a night & a half   running 3 terminals of the Dallas airport in heeled boots   on the cheapest layover you could find   love is asking   is waiting unnecessarily in the car until she is inside is H & their grown out fade   Victoria's babydoll dresses & pineapple hemp cigarettes   tobacco makes her head hurt   love is lifegiving & I am made of every girl who lent me shoes   Kavya with her wide smile & raven hair always pressing me to eat   Nina & her lipstick pink as tendon   watching a movie starring a Hutcherson   with our legs tangled together gossiping over mint tea   our laughter like a screen door in spring

The First Mermaid Ever Learns Imperial Units

iodide
exodus
idolize
nitrate
sulfate
ceremony
eulogy
hypnotize
monologue
prototype
melody
symbol
phenotype
method
metronome
protocol
homily
radio
odyssey
symbol
method
myth

I Wanna Be an Uncle When I Grow Up

we smoke on your balcony & joke about girls,
the kitchens we'd hide in. we share beers &
butter chicken & tangerine juice, the overpriced
sunset, & Palos Verdes is a wide, aromatic dream,
sidewalk hissing with salt. you advise me on
proper date etiquette & introduce me to 3arak,
reassure me I haven't ruined my life yet. you
reheat our favorite paella & set up the pillows
on the end of the sofa so we have back support.
we're always fighting something where our
spine meets the femur. we chose each other,
you & I. we debate which sugary drink to dam
our bellies with. it's Sunday & we're watching
The Office & I say I like Sprite the best it makes
me feel like I'm a hummingbird. your slow
breathing, your level voice after dinner. your hand
ruffling the top of my head while you laugh.

Staying in Touch with People Who Are Dead.

you remember, the vines were pressing too hard
on the plaster, & we were afraid she had—what was it?

                                                         lungs.

where do you keep your anger now?

                              shoulders + the rest
                                       in the navel.

that girl is still hungry as a dirge.
how much should we ask of her?

                        at least to feed the stray cats
              at midnight, burn something sweet, leave
          the window open so we can wander in.

I do prefer the lavender incense
to the patchouli shit.

                        & I hope she leaves some whiskey
                        on the altar soon. I'm tired of Tito's.

what's with the shaking?

                              my body's previous tenants
                                  forgot some terrors
                           I'm still trying to sanitize.
                            what was the glittering
                                   in your palms?

I was
carrying a flood.

Me & the Jinn in Your Laptop Had a Talk About You

>my mother always wore her blouses with the tags
tucked in. I tell the jinn I loved you that way, wary
even in the conditional. Marshall's on Grossmont
& the jinn offers me tulle that circles my waist like
calligraphy. I tell him I can't stop buying

>my clothes a little too small, that you look at me
like holy books. I tell him I wish our time
lingered as noon does after mass. the jinn offers
me parsley & vanilla extract to summon
your real name & mama leaves

>voicemails asking where I've disappeared. her
voice is a hymn suffusing the congregation's
shirts. the jinn in your house has seen my
eyes full of furniture for you, the acres
of velvet. it bothers me we have

>so many bones. you wear all two
hundred as if they are each
necessary. I want that certainty.
I want to be standing again
halfway cited in your room.

Horror Movie Where We Survive

you waltz through the bouquet of zombies
outside the Albertson's, skip pristine
sneakers over frankenstein feet. the dead

woman's gown is hissing, but it doesn't
matter. whatever happens next the annals
will conjugate. wear your most expensive

shoes, the dress with the long slit that makes
you feel like a good omen, bring the
locket full of teeth. scrawl the obituary in spit.

grief is like nicotine, it's a practice,
& despite the haunting, despite the history,
you reek of fever & lotus root, wrest

aloe vera peppermint elm from the dry
ground. you make the pavement bloom.
you build altars from soda bottles, cherry

pits, bobby pins, the wings of moths
not yet extinct. dial the headphones to
solange, let her sing you the sound of rain.

Pelvic Ultrasound in July

3 months & I haven't fixed you. now I'm a mother   so I   with my
womb sticking out. & my dress attracts bees. but I keep   /surprising myself.

      in a show I watched about a beautiful   daughter Lava
she'   high as shit.   had a nose like mine & hair crisp as   . at the end   the
handsome white protagonist tells their   *I don't need you*   but I
still   you. *do you want me?*   & the girlfriend had medium length hair & she said yes.
          you never asked.   always offered to feed   three times
     . by 9pm   convince each   to eat.   once   you were
frying shrimp on a quiet Thursday after work   you were so far away from me
I felt I might die just from that   if not the microplastics

    most of the women I've loved have been scientists. I wonder if this is a survival
instinct too.   at the beginning of August, I spend   two weeks
evening the tan on my breasts   I knew I loved it
because I hoped it would leave a mark.   when I was eight I saw
Haifa Wehbe on the television in a beige dress & mama clicked her tongue.   that
was when I realized I was a girl. a   .   . keresh. bzaz. kehss.
               to my secret. no language for a secret, or
        the way   trees sibling my legs. is my gender   chlorophyll?
air left alone from soldiers?
         & I walk around with my womb sticking out. you call me pretty in my
with dahlias on it.

Stations of the Cross

& god tugged my hair when I asked him

not to, proved
the twisting phonemes under my skin.

god still hasn't paid
his share of the rent & the couch is too small but sure. go ask a question.

و

you were tracing serifs into the dirt
with your sneakers, & He was arguing

on behalf of gravity. you drop the a's from your name

like seeds from a lemon rind. & god watches
all the iron it takes to slip

into your work clothes, the reflection
of your blurred halo in the gym. time

& death are cousins, lyrics
spilling from the leg press.

و

I found god
in the dregs of my purses, in bed with another song.

god & I are trying
to express gratitude more often so I let him

oracle my pillowcase for potential husbands & She
keeps my favorite Ajram poster hung on the wall.

As for Beauty, That Bitch with Her Hands in Our Larynx

I imagine she must have---

---I buy tongued underwear
in the shape of butterflies--

-------------------------------------the middle of---
October so the rain in California was just beginning to find its voice & I wore my veridian
Air Maxes ---

---sometimes I hate that I look like mom that way. I brush
back my ends which I tried solving with Pantene--

----------Exxon--

------------------Mielle. I landscape my heavy parts. I watch my sun in the mirror. I am a dying
----
------man. I am a--

---------------------------growing boy--

-----------------------who forgets to eat.--

Common Maronite Hymns

it's November & you don't want to leave the house, you smoked too much, but
she asked you to buy artichokes for dinner. you drive the refurbished Sentra
a healthy 40 & you buy 1 pound of spinach 2 cans of tuna & 3 men were made
into god. on your way out from the Kroger a god in a green Patagonia follows
you to the car. you walk fast & play Kendrick on the way home. you're 23 &
furious, sink teeming with parables, ironing her khakis in Ann Arbor, ignoring
calls at the Victoria Monet concert. let me try it unslant: when I was 13,
I used to watch the news counting how many of us had died. but you're 23
now; it's Euclid at 7 o'clock & you're wearing too-tight denim at the Buddha
Trixie show your sister dragged you to & the metal in your mouth becomes
bass, elbows pressing into the skinny dudes surrounding you, dread just for
the sake of dread, white boy unhappiness, sweaty & lightly refreshing, like
a really good Coke. but it's still November & there is her smile, getting the car
ready for the oil change. you wanted to stay home but there was a beautiful girl
with her index in your cervix, & you were writing a song about god.

Music to Drown By

we sing for weeks. we sing until the empire is over, until the moon runs out of neighbors, until the horizon ends its affair with verse. we sing until we make poetry, until we are the beauty prophets warn about. we sing, bangles dripping with dishwater. we sing monstrous, sing the myth of our continued living from mother to daughter. we sing because we know our ghosts & they like when some tarab gets in the mashawi. we sing kneeling before our figurines of the Virgin, we sing chewing dates, rolling grape leaves, our wrists winding riverine, our ululations loud & combing thick black braids of helixed hair. we sing for the boys who died in the jnoub, for the women who disappeared on the outskirts of Beirut & Hama & Kafroun, we make them a place in our singing, we sing for the dayy3at & their names before the Crusades. we make the room simmer like a school of bream. we shrug verdant maquis over our shoulders, we remember the holy places on the hills, we sing until our blood has meaning again. we insist on Sundays & in the middle of the week & after midnight kyrie eleison kyrie eleison kyrie eleison. we sing because we want to make the oceans bluer & the children more innocent. we sing with the cadence of all our aunties, of all god's daughters smoking mint apple shisha & we henna our arms with the outlines of jasmine & we let daylight refine our voices. we make moss with our hips, reforest the barren fields with our stubbornness. we sing & we fill our singing with murex shells, our bountiful & purple language, we sing until marrow, muscle, ligament, myth. may peace be upon you. & we make it.

Acknowledgments

Thank you to the journals listed below for homing previous versions of these poems:

Diode Poetry Journal, "Analgesic"
Gulf Coast, "Archive Spilled on Entryway"
Michigan Quarterly Review, "Haggling the Shami Way"
Mizna, "Pelvic Ultrasound in July"
Muzzle Magazine, "In Which Every Day I Get More Lovely Regardless of My Early Onset" and "Mitosis"
The Offing, "The First Mermaid Climbs Out the Sea," "Excerpt from September," and "Anatomy of Gati's Vanity"
Only Poems, "Amtrak Devotional," "$40 Beige Rico Nasty Tee," "I Wanna Be an Uncle When I Grow Up," and "Pleasure Is Data"
Palette Poetry, "Aubade with Lobotomized Mountain"
Poetry Magazine, "How to Braid an Artery"
The Sewanee Review, "Estuary Ghazal (Arab)"

Notes

"Aubade with Lobotomized Mountain" is inspired by Kaveh Akbar's poem "River of Milk" (*Poetry*, October 2016).

The research referenced in "Excerpts from September's Effects" is from Aloud and Rathur's 2009 article, *Factors Affecting Attitudes Toward Seeking and Using Formal Mental Health and Psychological Services Among Arab Mulis Populations*, 4 J. Muslim Mental Health 79, 79–103, https://doi.org/10.1080/15564900802487675.

The quote in "The First Mermaid Ever" is from chapter 8 of Glueck's Registration Book, "The Nabatean Temple at Khirbet Et-Tannur, Jordan: Volume 2—Cultic Offerings, Vessels, And Other Specialist Reports," Judith McKenzie, ed. The coin image is from Nicholas Wright's article, "Non-Greek Religious Imagery on the Coinage of Seleucid Syria," *Mediterranean Archaeology* 22/23 (2009/10): 193–206.

"Haptic" is a golden shovel taking the last words of a section from Threa Almontaser's poem "Hidden Bombs in My Coochie," specifically, "the news makes me touch / myself find the panic / button of my body / & press hard."

In "GATI.fm," the phrase "made a fandroid outta your girlfriend" is lifted from Janelle Monáe's 2018 song "Django Jane."

"Annotated Bibliography" is a cento composed entirely of lines borrowed from, in order: Mohammed El-Kurd's *Perfect Victims And the Politics of Appeal*; Munira Khayyat's *A Landscape of War: Ecologies of Resistance and Survival in South Lebanon*; Safia Elhillo's *Bright Red Fruit*; Mona Chalabi's "Who Profits From Killing?"; Jasbir Puar's *Terrorist Assemblages: Homonationalism in Queer Times*; Mona Chalabi's "Who Profits From Killing?"; Etel Adnan's *Of Cities and Women (Letters to Fawwaz)*; Mejdulene Shomali's *Between Banat: Queer Arab Critique and Transnational Arab Archives*; Munira Khayyat's *A Landscape of War*; Predrag Matvejević's *Mediterranean Breviary*; Mari-Lou Rowley's *Catastrophe Theories*; and Tarik Dobbs's *Nazar Boy*.

The image and caption on page 22 is from the Library of Congress's Matson Photograph Collection, titled "Along the Coast to Tripoli. Tripoli. El-Bedoui. Seething Mass of 'Sacred Fish.'"

The first quote in "Haggling the Shami Way" is from Sennah Yee's poem "Bond 'Girls' Pt.1: Lucia." The second quote is from page 50 of Etel Adnan's *Of Cities and Women*, in her letter from Murcia, dated November 10, 1990.

The line "is my uterus / compostable? & who the fuck took my pearls? in "Ritual Ethnography" is lifted from Anastacia-Renée's poem "Retrofuckery," from her book *Side Notes from the Archivist*. The quote from the Bible referenced on the second page of the poem is from Ecclesiastes 7:17, which says, "Do not be overly wicked, and do not be a fool—why die before your time?".

The show referenced in "Pelvic Ultrasound in July" is *Feel Good* on Netflix.

The final version of "Music to Drown By" owes its development to Aracelis Girmay's poem "& When We Woke."

Gratitudes

To my sister and brother—everything I make is for you. Thank you, Nina, for being my sister in every sense of the word. I am impossible without you. Anthony, you keep me young. I am grateful to my grandmother Esperanza for watching over me and always keeping me in touch with my gut. Thank you to my chosen sisters: Huong Nguyen, Haewon Ma, Ayisha Siddiqa, Blaine Samson, and Andrea Morales.

Thank you to Amelia Crowther for her meticulous, lovely attention to this book in its first stages, and to Taylor Byas for her essential feedback and insights as this book grew up. I could not have made this creature without you both. Thank you to Maya Marshall for believing in this book, and for being such a wonderfully clear and curious editor. Thank you to the Sewanee Writers' Conference (and the RAWI fellowship that made my attendance there possible), the Bread Loaf Environmental Writers' Conference, the Tin House Writers's Workshop, and the National Endowment for the Arts for providing space and support for this book's development.

My writing exists with eternal gratitude to the brilliant poets I've had the honor to learn from: Safia Elhillo, Fady Joudah, Hayan Charara, Keith Wilson, Victoria Chang, Nate Marshall, Marianne Chan, Taylor Byas, KB Brookins, and Anthony Cody. I am also grateful to the work of the following visionary poets, whose work has changed how I think, write and dream: Hala Alyan, Maram Al-Massri, Nizar Qabbani, Danez Smith, Vanessa Villareal, Solmaz Sharif, Adonis, Franny Choi, Summer Farah, and Noor Hindi. I remain indebted to the thinking of our theorists, especially Edward Said, Jasbir Puar, Achille Mbembe, Mejdulene Shomali, and Frantz Fanon. Of course, thank you to Haifa Wehbe, the original Arab bad girl.

This book would not be possible without some north star inspirations, which I hope the work lives in cousinhood with: Sennah Yee's *How Do I Look?*; the movie *Atlantics*; Banah el Ghadbanah's *La Syrena: Visions of a Syrian Mermaid from Space*; Etel Adnan's writing, especially *The Arab Apocalypse* and *Of Cities and Women: Letters to Fawwaz*; Munira Khayyat's *A Landscape of War*; Ariana Benson's *Black Pastoral*; Hala Alyan's *The Arsonists' City*; and Rochelle Jordan's music, especially her fourth album. You can find the book playlist at mayasalameh.com.

To a free Palestine, Syria, Lebanon. To a future where my people can learn, play, and be, from the river to the sea. May we never forget.

About the Author

Photo credit: Ryan Wimsatt

Maya Salameh is the author of *How to Make an Algorithm in the Microwave* (University of Arkansas Press, 2022), winner of the Etel Adnan Poetry Prize and finalist for the California Book Award. Salameh is the recipient of a National Endowment for the Arts Poetry Fellowship, the Markowitz Award for Exceptional New Writers, and the Sewanee Review Poetry Prize. She has received support from the Tin House Writers' Workshop, Sewanee Writers' Conference, Bread Loaf Environmental Writers' Conference, and the President's Committee for the Arts and Humanities. Her work has appeared in *The Offing*, *Poetry*, *Gulf Coast*, *The Rumpus*, *AGNI*, *Mizna*, and the *LA Times*. She is a JD candidate at UCLA School of Law. She can be found at @mayaslmh or mayasalameh.com.

About Haymarket Poetry

Haymarket Poetry celebrates inventive, insightful, and rigorous poetry and creative nonfiction at the intersection of art and politics, particularly from a diverse array of writers whose books both feed and emerge from social movements. In the tradition of June Jordan and Sonia Sanchez, ours is a liberatory poetics. We publish poems to change the world.

We publish daring, radical artists like Eve L. Ewing, aja monet, Mohammed El-Kurd, José Olivarez, Nate Marshall, Mahogany L. Browne, George Abraham, and other leading writers of our time.

We are home to a diverse array of socially conscious, music-forward poetry anthologies and collections, and series bringing art and analysis to the fore.

HAYMARKET POETRY BOARD

Maya Marshall, poetry editorial director
Camonghne Felix, advisor
Cortney Lamar Charleston, advisor
Aurielle Marie Lucier, advisor
Jameka Williams, production editor

About Haymarket Books

Haymarket Books is radically independent. We seek to drive a wedge into the risk-averse world of corporate book publishing. Haymarket also manages a vibrant community organizing and event space in Chicago, Haymarket House; the popular Haymarket Books Live event series and podcast; and the annual Socialism Conference.

www.ingramcontent.com/pod-product-compliance
Lightning Source LLC
Jackson TN
JSHW071238200226
98336JS00004B/12

Praise for *Mermaid Theory*

This collection is a delight of dream logic, old and new mythologies, intimacies, and hallucinatory sciences. I will read anything Maya Salameh writes. *Mermaid Theory* is awash with newness, with wonder.

—Safia Elhillo, author of *Girls That Never Die: Poems*

What I enjoy about Maya Salameh's poems in *Mermaid Theory* is the surprise. Every sentence in these poems is an opportunity to see something differently, to astonish. Just a few examples: "in the house we speak 3 languages but grooming's the first," "I'll transcribe myself / to bricks," or "it's November now / & the noun under the sink is screaming again." Formally inventive, imagistically surprising, and intellectually capacious and nuanced, *Mermaid Theory* skillfully explores mythology, Arab American identity and womanhood, faith, and so much more.

—Victoria Chang, author of *With My Back to the World: Poems*

From Syria to the house party, there is no landscape that Maya Salameh cannot paint with rigorous spirit, delectable lyric, and a fierce poetics all her own. At times sexy and lush as a Prince song, at other times singing in the righteous harmonies of necessary revolutions, *Mermaid Theory* breathes the wonder of myth into the poet's witnessing of the worlds around her. The result is a book you won't want to put down—a book that demands to be read aloud with friends, a book that feels like a warm room where your best girls are waiting for you to arrive. Everywhere here there is love, so much love that the poet must confess, "of all / my prayers you are my favorite." So much love hums off these pages that "this song / lasts longer than the mountains & all the horses nearby can smell it." A truly fantastic collection that begs to be savored over and over.

—Danez Smith, author of *Bluff: Poems*

Formally daring and politically incisive, *Mermaid Theory* reckons with water as history, as present, as divinity, as desire, as fear—as at once "a vast archive" and "an immense grave." Refusing cultural amnesia and feel-good liberal sentimentality, these poems read "the dead's grammar" and praise a "ravenous love for life." This is a poet who is not waiting around for the imperialist death machine to declare who counts as a person or what counts as art. This is a poet who sings from the river to the sea. Maya Salameh knows that to write is to "sing until the empire is over."

—Chen Chen, author of *Your Emergency Contact Has Experienced an Emergency*

Maya Salameh's *Mermaid Theory* is a precise and intimate book about girlhood, the body, and what it means to grow up in a world that is neither kind nor forgiving. These poems move between memory, inheritance, and the daily negotiations of becoming, holding tenderness and harm in the same frame. Salameh writes with clarity about girlhood as both a site of imagination and constraint, where myth, family, and history quietly shape the self. I love this book and am dazzled by its sharpness, its humor, and its depth.

—Noor Hindi, coeditor of *Heaven Looks Like Us: Palestinian Poetry*

Mermaid Theory is luscious and lilting, softly chaotic and fierce. I savored every word of this testament to the messy tendrils of desire, sex, war, and creative embodiment. Gorgeous libidinal energy radiates off every page of this exquisite collection—a truly beautiful body of work.

—Jasbir Puar, author of *The Right to Maim: Debility, Capacity, Disability*

Maya Salameh is an intelligent, daring poet sculpting her art between the irreverent and the experimental. *Mermaid Theory* propels the imaginary toward movement. This is cinema in verse.

—Fady Joudah, author of *[...]*